How To Sift Through Media Bullsh*t

A Quick Guide

Written By

Bo Bennett, PhD

Prefer video? Take the online video-based course at

www.VirversitY.com/ courses/consumeinfo

eBookIt.com
365 Boston Post Road, #311
Sudbury, MA 01776

First printing - April 2017
Paperback Version 1.0 Aug 18, 2018

publishing@ebookit.com
http://www.ebookit.com

Copyright 2017, eBookIt.com
ISBN: 978-1-4566-3192-5

Table of Contents

Preface

A fact is a fact, right? Unfortunately, it's not that simple. A "fact" is primarily defined as "a thing that is indisputably the case." The problem with that definition is that virtually anything can be disputed, and most things are. But the legal language of "beyond a reasonable doubt" applies to this definition. Many times, especially on the Internet, facts that are disputed are done so WITHOUT reasonable doubt. For example, there is an entire organization devoted to disputing the fact that the earth is NOT flat.

A secondary definition of "fact" is "a piece of information used as evidence or as part of a report or news article." These "facts" are still "things that are indisputably the case," or are supposed to be, but used in this context; facts are used to support a theory, conclusion, or opinion. For example, one might argue that the government is out to enslave its citizens. They may offer several facts to support that argument including the facts that the government can imprison people, the government has imprisoned people, and the government has no plans to stop imprisoning people. No reasonable person would dispute those facts, but that doesn't mean that the facts adequately support the argument or claim.

Very little information we consume is straight fact. We consume opinion, commentary, satire, gossip, conspiracy theories, marketing copy, and other forms of non-facts. Even when we are given facts, it can be done in such way to mislead, deceive, and manipulate where we are led to develop a false sense of confidence in our conclusions based on these facts.

Oh, by the way, "alternative facts," are falsehoods.

In this book, we will go over important concepts that will help you to become a more responsible consumer of information including:

• Important terms such as fake news site, click bait, echo chamber, and more.

• How our cognitive biases get in the way when it comes to accepting reality.

• How to quickly evaluate any information source.

• How to ask the right questions when deciding how much weight to give information.

• How to spot when you are being misled, deceived, manipulated, or outright lied to.

We may not have a legal obligation when it comes to being a responsible consumer of information. But one can easily argue that we do have a moral obligation. A society is only as good as its citizens, and our intellectual contributions or lack thereof have far-reaching effects. While this short book is unlikely to make you a master of parsing information, it's a heck of a good start!

Bo Bennett, PhD

LESSON 1: Know Your Own Biases

Let's not pretend objective facts don't exist and everything is up for debate. In practical terms (not bizarrely philosophical terms), there are things that are simply true, no matter how many people deny them. For example, a bachelor can't be married, it can't get any colder than absolute zero, and Steve Martin's Roxanne is the best movie of all time. Alright, that last one's an opinion... but it should be a fact! But facts make up a very small portion of all our information. The media today is chock full of information but scarce on facts. Is Donald Trump the greatest President in the history of the United States? Is America the greatest country in the world? Should the use and sale of marijuana be decriminalized at the federal level? The answers to these questions are not facts, although they should be supported by facts. We can all be exposed to the same facts, yet come to wildly different conclusions. But why?

We're not blank slates. We all bring to the table a lifetime of values, beliefs, and background information that play a big part in how we interpret new information. Also, our brains are not wired for reason; they're wired for procreation and survival. This results in us taking mental shortcuts to conserve cognitive energy at the expense of reason. This phenomenon is demonstrated through what are known as cognitive biases. In this lesson, we'll go over ten of the most problematic cognitive biases when it comes to consuming information. The reason we're doing this, is because the most effective way to combat our own biases is to be aware of them.

1. **Availability heuristic.** This is the tendency to overestimate the likelihood of events with greater "availability" in memory, which can be influenced by how recent the memories are or how unusual or emotionally charged they may be. Most people who are terrified of being killed by terrorists don't lose a moment of sleep about being killed by lightning, even though they are many times more likely to die from being struck by lightning. Terrorist attacks are emotionally-charged events that, as wrong as it sounds, have high entertainment value. When they occur, these events dominate the media for days, and sometimes months (like in the case of 9/11). Based on this level of exposure, our emotions overpower our reasoning and what is factually a statistical impossibility becomes a perceived "strong possibility." This bias affects our views on other issues such as white cops killing unarmed black men if you consume more liberal media, or acts of heroism by cops if you consume mostly

conservative media. Besides making sure you get your information from an array of credible sources, realize that ALL media reports on information that is interesting or entertaining, which skews our perception of the world.

2. **Availability cascade.** This is a self-reinforcing process in which a collective belief gains more and more plausibility through its increasing repetition in public discourse (or "repeat something long enough, and it will become true"). Surrounding yourself with biased news sources is known as creating your own "echo chamber," where you hear the same views that largely go unchallenged. The more your hear them, the more you believe them, regardless of the amount or quality of evidence that is provided. This is why getting your information from balanced sources is extremely important. If you like the political commentary and can't get by on the associate press-style facts alone, choose both a left and right wing source of political commentary. This is an effective technique for combatting this bias.

3. **Belief bias.** This is an effect where someone's evaluation of the logical strength of an argument is biased by the believability of the conclusion. So if you are already

convinced that politician "A" is corrupt, then the assertions made with no supporting evidence about politician A's corruption is far more likely to be believed, even though such a belief is unwarranted due to the lack of evidence. This makes manipulating and selling falsehoods to already strongly biased information consumers, dangerously easy. Ask yourself *why* do you find something believable? The chances are, you formed that belief more on emotion than reason.

4.   **Bias blind spot.** This is the tendency to see oneself as less biased than other people or to be able to identify more cognitive biases in others than in oneself. We see this often in social media comments when accusations of bias and fallacies are indiscriminately dished out or when certain media outlets or politicians are quick to point out the biases of other media outlets or politicians while being under the false illusion that they are the only ones that are truly "fair and balanced." Realize that you do have biases. The more you realize this, the less problematic this bias will be—and ironically, the less biased you will become.

5.   **Confirmation bias.** This is the motherload of cognitive biases. This is the tendency to search for, interpret, focus on, and remember information in a way that

confirms one's preconceptions. In this context, this affects what sources we go to for information. We like when reality agrees with us, not when it disagrees with us, so if we have a strong belief that lizard people are ruling the planet in secret, we might choose to get our news from such sources that promote this idea (and yes, there are several). The confirmation bias also helps us to conveniently "forget" those facts that contradict our views, and at the same time, helps us to remember all the information that supports our views. Be committed to the truth, no matter what that truth may be. This will help mitigate this bias.

6. **Dunning–Kruger effect.** This is the tendency for unskilled individuals to overestimate their own ability and the tendency for experts to underestimate their own ability. This effect can best be summed up in the statement "Please do not confuse your Google search with my PhD." Experts in fields have more than facts; they are able to synthesize facts and information to come to conclusions that are far more probable than conclusions drawn from those who have the same facts but lack the understanding of the facts and the academic field in which those facts exist. Experts are

wrong, but non-experts are wrong far more often.

7. **Halo effect.** This is the tendency for a person's positive or negative traits to "spill over" from one personality area to another in others' perceptions of them. Our political party's leaders often become untouchable heroes to us that can do no wrong. We might deify them initially for any single reason, but then through the halo effect, interpret all of their policies, actions, behaviors, skills, and social media posts as positive, despite strong evidence to the contrary.

8. **Identifiable victim effect.** This is the tendency to respond more strongly to a single identified person at risk than to a large group of people at risk. When charities ask us for our money, they usually don't just tell us that X percent of people are suffering; they show us a single victim with which we can emotionally identify. This type of prosocial manipulation is mostly harmless when used by charities, but it is a major problem when used by media sources or individuals who choose to mostly share stories about a single victim as a way to make the problem appear much worse than it actually is. Sure, it seems wrong treating people as statistics, but unless we look at global and national problems statistically,

we can be distracted from much bigger problems that need our attention.

9. **Illusory truth effect.** This is the tendency to believe that a statement is true if it is easier to process, or if it has been stated multiple times, regardless of its actual veracity. These are specific cases of truthiness. Similar to the availability cascade, the more we hear a lie, the more likely we are to accept it as truth. But this also has to do with how easy the information is to process. When a politician says "I am going to fix the healthcare problems and make our system the best in the world," we tend to believe this because of its simplicity. If the same politician were to precisely explain what he or she will fix, using legal and economics jargon, that message is less likely to be believed. Sometimes the truth is simple, but sometimes it's not.

10. **Subjective validation.** Through subjective validation, a person will consider a statement or another piece of information to be correct if it has any personal meaning or significance to them. This explains why so many people believe in horoscopes, astrological signs, palm readings, and spam e-mails that appear to have the solution to their problems. Through subjective validation, it is easy for an information

source to convince us that a series of unrelated events are related, which often form the foundation for irrational conspiracy theories. Be on the lookout for ambiguous claims that can apply to anyone or any situation. For example, a horoscope telling you that you are "someone who likes spending time with others, but also appreciates time alone."

Again, simply being aware of these biases is a great start to mitigating their negative effects. In the next lesson, we will look at sources of information, specifically how to know on which ones you can rely and which ones you cannot.

LESSON 2: Know the Source

Imagine someone told you that they were abducted by aliens and got to travel the universe. Would you believe them? Before you answer that, you should be asking how credible is this person? Do they have a history of making stuff up? Have they ever lied to you before? Do I even know this person? But even then, based on the extraordinary nature of the claim, you should demand a higher standard of evidence before believing in the claim. Even if this person never lied to you before, the person can just be mistaken—lying isn't the only possibility.

With the alien abduction story in mind, if you read something on the Internet that was not as extraordinary as being taking for a ride around the universe by aliens, but still surprising nonetheless, you want to ask similar questions. How reliable is this source? What evidence do they present to support their claim? Even if you are getting this information from a trusted news source, you want to apply a healthy dose of skepticism—especially to claims that are out of the ordinary.

First, some basic information about the media. Whether we're talking about a major network, a publicly-funded station, a college newspaper, a lone blogger, or a friend sharing a story on social media, if the information run, posted, or shared is not appreciated by others, that information source will eventually stop sharing that kind of information. We tend to blame the media for much of what they share, yet we are equally responsible for supporting such sources with our subscriptions, donations, views, shares, likes, and comments. If you want to do your part in improving the quality of information available, stop supporting these garbage sources. Yes, even a comment on their site or post expressing your disapproval keeps them in business. This is one case where if we ignore our problems, they will go away.

There are two more terms that you need to know: "fake news" and "clickbait." No, fake news is not defined as news you disagree with. Calling a source "fake news" because they said something you didn't like about your political party is like calling a white couple "racist" because they gave birth to a white baby. Fake news websites deliberately publish hoaxes, propaganda, and disinformation purporting to be real news. Even if MSNBC or FOX News gets a story a wrong, it is highly unlikely that such news would qualify as "fake news." Fake news websites specialize in fake news.

Click bait is content whose main purpose is to attract attention and encourage visitors to click on a link to a particular web page. Headlines such as "Does this photo really show [insert good-looking movie star here] naked on a nude beach?" Then, once you click on the link, you discover three things: 1) you are bombarded with ads, often to the point where your browser crashes, 2) No, that was not a photo of the good-looking movie star nude on the beach (it was an old guy in a beige Speedo) and 3) you're a sucker. Here's a hint: if you see click bait headlines in social media, and you really are tempted to click the link, read the comments. There were likely many suckers before you who will share the "big reveal" with you in the comments.

There are many categories of information sources. The ones we are mostly focusing on in this book are online media sources including major news outlets, websites, blogs, and those who share information via social media. But there are also encyclopedias, academic sources, first-hand accounts, gossip, offline media, and more. To make things more complicated, there are subcategories of each source. For example, within major news outlets, we can break them down to fact reporting outlets such as Reuters or the Associated Press or political commentaries such as FOX News and MSNBC. And even individual sources can be a mix of fact-reporting, commentary, satire, fake news, tabloid style, and investigative journalism. The bottom line is, the more you know about what kind of source you're dealing with, as well as how biased the source is, the better prepared you will be to apply an appropriate level of skepticism to the information shared by the source.

So how do we apply skepticism when it comes to evaluating the credibility of information?

• **What is the point, argument, or claim?** Often people just like to ramble and don't necessarily have a point, argument, or claim. Sometimes articles or commentary are indirectly making claims under the guise of asking questions. For example, you might see the headline, "Was Obama REALLY born in the US?" If that is all you see, the headline clearly was designed to get clicks as well as spread doubt about Obama's birthplace. The article might continue with a series of questions, not making a single claim, or citing a single source.

• **What's the source?** Most sources have biases —political, religious, ideological, or otherwise. What are your favorite sources of information? As objectively as possible, think about the sources biases. You can research media bias and see independent reports by nonpartisan, non-profit groups. Don't fall for the "mainstream media is evil" narrative that is so often perpetuated by lesser-known sources that desperately want their share of viewers. This is not unlike cult behavior where cult leaders attempt to discredit people who attempt call attention to the fact that they are a cult. Instead of telling you to only associate with cult members, these media sources will tell you that you can only trust them, and all other sources should be avoided. Multiple narratives and viewpoints are the path to being a responsible consumer of information; it's not the refusal to hear and consider other viewpoints.

- **Who's the author?** A big red flag is raised when an article or source of information is anonymous. Credible news sources have staff journalists who proudly put their name on their work. Like a good source, there are good journalists who can generally be trusted based on their history of work. The problem is, when an article, post, video, or other form of information is signed "staff" or some other generic entity, or not signed at all, there is no one who is being held accountable for the information. And don't be deceived by fake author names. Look the author up. It is not difficult to see if they are a real person or not.

- **How are the terms being defined?** A headline might read "Finally, PROOF of Life After Death." What is meant by "proof"? What is meant by "life after death"? In this case, "proof" meant a story by a child and "life after death" meant a dream-like experience while the child's heart stopped, but brain activity was still strong.

- **Is this a fact or an opinion?** There is a big difference between the two, and very often opinions are sold as facts. If it is actually a fact, does the evidence adequately support the claim? If it is an opinion, has the opinion been adequately supported by facts?

- **What is the date of the story?** Recycled stories tend to make their way around social media when they are more meaningful. For example, if a vote is coming up on gun control, people will find stories from the last decade about kids getting shot accidentally, or hero citizens with a gun that shot the bad guy and saved the day. This gives the false impression that these events are more common than they actually are.

- **Are you reading more than the headline?** If you are going to accept any information, don't stop at the headline. As we have seen and will see more of in the next lesson, headlines are notoriously manipulative, even with the most reputable sources.

- **Did you follow the evidence?** One great advantage of getting information on the Internet is the ability to fact check in real time. If the information is an article, see if facts are cited or linked. For example, if a science reporter is writing about the outcome of a study, is the study linked to the article? It should be—or at least cited in the references. Be very skeptical of assertions made or supposed facts mentioned with no trail leading to the source. When you follow the sources to the original source, what you often find is that you were an unwilling participant in a game of telephone, where the information you have is significantly different from the information in the original source. A recent example is all those articles claiming that a glass of wine is better for you than an hour at the gym. Of course, this was a serious distortion of the conclusion made by the original researchers involved in the study.

A good rule of thumb is to simply check multiple sources. Ask yourself, how come the major networks aren't reporting this information? And remember, extraordinary claims require extraordinary evidence. If Bill the blogger claims the government is run by lizard people, and the reason you won't hear about this on the major networks, is because the major networks are also run by lizard people, then before accepting such a conspiracy, make sure you have enough evidence to support the conspiracy.

Bo Bennett, PhD

LESSON 3: Know When You Are Being Misled, Deceived, Manipulated, or Outright Lied To

A "lie" is only the tip of the metaphorical iceberg when it comes to things that are not true. Misinformation comes in many forms, and in this lesson, I'll show you how to spot some of the most common ways people are misled, deceived, manipulated, and outright lied to.

Opinion or commentary, not facts.

People are often misled when opinion or commentary is being sold as fact. This is often the case with political commentators who appear to have the authority of news anchors, yet can say whatever they want without having to support their claims or preface them with "in my opinion." There is nothing wrong with opinion or commentary, as long as we recognize it as such and don't mistake it for fact reporting.

Selective reporting.

Media outlets lie by omission and demonstrate their biased worldview by only running stories that comport with their biases and agenda. With this technique, we can make anyone look like a monster or a saint, without technically lying. Sometimes stories cannot be ignored, but media outlets can present just one side of the story and do so in a biased way. They can hold back relevant facts and tell "half-truths." Similarly, one can focus on what did happen and leave out what didn't happen, or vice versa.

Misleading proportionality.

Media outlets can give the impression that with any issue where there is an overwhelming scientific consensus that legitimate controversy exists. They do this by giving "equal time" to those with outlier ideas. For example, although roughly 97% of climatologists agree on climate change, a media outlet might focus on the 3% who don't. This technique also helps cast doubt on facts. By giving equal time to people who deny facts, "alternative facts" are born.

Creating stereotypes.

A very common form of media manipulation is when an author suggests that one person's actions are representative of their group when this one person is an outlier. For example, a conservative press might run a story about a feminist who thinks all men should be killed and suggests through careful wording, that this one person is representative of all feminists. This also occurs when qualifiers such as "all, most, some, none," or "every" are conveniently ignored when making a claim about a group. For example, "Republicans hate Mexicans." All Republicans? Without a qualifier, either "all" or "most" can be assumed, when sometimes it should "some," "a small percentage of," or even just "a couple."

Ambiguity.

The use of ambiguous, emotionally-charged words with little or no substance is a common method of deceit and manipulation. This is like a politician emotionally shouting, "I support freedom and the American way of life!" What the heck does that mean? How does that translate to actual policies? Perhaps she means she wants to free all prisoners? Perhaps she means she wants to lock up many more people so other citizens can be "free" from concern of harm? As long as specifics are left out, people are free to read in their own meanings, which very often leads to political polarization.

Suggest, imply, but don't directly state.

"Are you a doctor?" "Wow, you are very perceptive!" "What kind of doctor are you?" "I'm not a doctor." "But you said you were a doctor?" "No, I didn't. You said I was a doctor. I just said that you were perceptive." Suggesting and implying is common in most forms of communication as a "shortcut", but this is also often abused to absolve the communicator from any legal responsibility while still indirectly making their claim. Don't be afraid to ask for clarity or an affirmative or negative statement related to your question, and don't stop asking until you get a clear answer.

Ambiguous Pervasiveness.

If one wants something to appear more frequent or pervasive than it actually is, one just needs to make an ambiguous statement such as "People all over the world believe in a flat earth." Technically, this is true. There might be a few people on each continent (and hundreds in America) that believe this. But "people all over the world" sounds like there are more of them than there actually are. Another example is saying something such as "Animosity against postal workers is problem." Perhaps two postal workers were attacked in the last year because they were postal workers. Sure, even one attack it too many, but stating "Animosity against postal workers is problem" implies much greater pervasiveness than is reflected in reality.

Labeling.

Don't be so quick to accept labels others apply to people and ideas. If people are called "racist" or "bigoted," and such labels aren't immediately justified with evidence, ignore the labels rather than parroting them. The same goes for labels given to ideas and events. Usually, these labels are given out of emotion and not reason. Perhaps that latest decided court case was a "miscarriage of justice," but find out why it was a "miscarriage of justice" if the information source got lazy and didn't bother telling you why.

Deflecting.

This is a common technique in debate or in an adversarial interview where the interviewer will ask the interviewee a question, and the interviewee will "deflect" by asking the interviewer a question, changing the subject, or otherwise simply not answering the question. Good interviewers won't let their interviewee's get away with this, but many do. Don't be satisfied with a non-answer, and especially, don't assume the answer you want to hear.

Exaggeration or Minimisation.

Some people are more prone to exaggeration than others. Exaggeration is usually accompanied by ambiguous words such as "greatest," "best," "smartest," but can also be falsifiable claims such as "I won by the biggest margin ever." *Minimisation* is the opposite of exaggeration where the enormity or seriousness is grossly understated.

"Just joking."

Humor is wonderful, and sites like "The Onion" are hilarious. The problem is when humor becomes more passive-aggressive or when it is unclear that humor is being used. When people are proven wrong, claiming they were "just joking" or "being sarcastic" is one way to avoid taking responsibility for their false claims.

Puffery.

Puffery is frequently used in marketing. It is defined as "exaggerated commendation especially for promotional purposes." So when you see a sign that says "World's best cup of coffee," don't be like Buddy the Elf and assume that it really is the world's best cup of coffee. It's probably just a crappy cup of coffee.

Accusation with no evidence.

Unfortunately, this is very common, especially with less-reputable media sources or individuals who aren't known for their honesty. This is common because an accusation alone can change the minds of the public, regardless of the facts. People have had their lives destroyed by being falsely accused of a heinous crime. When the person is vindicated, very often the visceral disgust that was felt for the person does not go away. Don't accept accusations lightly—demand evidence.

Quotes out of context / fake quotes.

Headlines that interpret words of a person while still using quotes can be incredibly deceptive. For example, "Politician X: murdering people is fun." This headline clearly implies that politician X said that murdering people is fun. So what did politician

X actually say? Once you dig deeper (which very few people do), you will see that the actual quote was "Violent crime is a major problem that needs to be addressed. Many criminals murdered people because it gives them an adrenaline rush—a kind of high without needing drugs." Not quite the same, is it?

Claim causation where there is only correlation.

This is common with the social justice movement, where "racism," "sexism," "transphobia," "xenophobia" or other -isms and phobias are said to be responsible for actions or problems, where no such causation has been established.

Use of anecdotes.

In science, anecdotes are among the worse form of "evidence," yet outside of science, they are used all the time because they have a strong emotional appeal. Facts to don't stand a chance to a strong, emotional anecdote. For example, evidence strongly supports the safety and necessity of vaccines. But all it takes is one story of a child who had a bad adverse reaction from a vaccine to change public opinion on the overall safety of vaccines.

What other ways do providers of information mislead, deceive, manipulate, and outright lie to us? Think about this question the next time you're surfing the Internet, going through your social media feeds, watching television, reading the newspaper, or otherwise consuming information. Critical thinking requires that you don't automatically accept information, but that you apply a healthy dose of skepticism when it comes to deciding which information to accept, and which to reject. The more you practice this, the better you'll get.

Did you like this information? Check out the online course at

https://www.VirversitY.com/courses/consumeinfo

Help us to share this course and make the world a more reasonable place!